Day's Afternoon

Poems for Days

Patrick Playter Hartigan

Double Movement Publications

ISBN: 978-0-615-25077-9

Design, production, and illustration by Patrick Playter Hartigan

Cover Illustration: *Days*, August, 2008, graphite stick and oil stick on paper, by Patrick Playter Hartigan

Double Movement Publications
Patrick Playter Hartigan
2239 SE 47th Avenue
Portland, Oregon, 97215

Contents

For Endi and Jackson

Day's Afternoon

Days

What did you do today? And
if today has served others
- how is my life composed?

An original day drawn from
the hip of a day retiring,
& between us, a world, say

From the sky falls an army
of silver and black days -
marigolds crushed in lines

Or men and women inventing
days about casually in the
evenings of other plunder.

What do I know? What can I
contribute to a discussion
transparent and under way?

I have a day in one hand &
in the other one that fits
the first's disappearances

Both are responsibly clear
tinged with eluding yellow
- but calm in my open hand

Onto work - and me holding
one day and the other, and
unwilling to ask for help:

Here comes someone to help
Here is a woman to hold my
hands Days I cannot forget

What did you ask me first?
Can I say what I do, or do
the days fall to patterns?

The easy part is I am near
a reckoning, water swiftly
catches at the passing air

The harder part is all the
reckoning past: I have not
amounted to one who sleeps

for pleasure. Simple earth
- your tales & transparent
workings - what do you do?

Some Returns

1.

Air from the North pressed
on pillowed heads Darkness
mute @ a mechanistic labor

2.

Into th' car then you and I
where fingers start @ road
side contraptions or paint

3.

Money into a bank the bank
into a body that body into
a street broken at the sea

4.

Like a journey in a book -
like a journey I can read:
red petals from warm water

5.

Darkness decided and still
and into a corner this man
counting @ columns of gold

6.

We said run a lot and said
stop when we decided to We
fell into each others arms

At Home

This is a kind of play
No an accident No this
is blood No bone These
are threads No tenants
No it's a kind of home
No factory No you have
no property This is my
property No This is no
work This is anybody's
business No I mean yes
Yes You are my anybody

Day Counter

I am the simplest person
you know. I can say only
what words comprehend. I
am apparent and relevant

A heart and my histories
are a redundany of where
I wrote from and what we
were feeling at the time

You will not say poetry.
I cannot allow it. Whole
cloth it was and remains
so what mattered is pure

because we found it. Our
hope, too, blistered, is
known beyond recognition
- it all ends in the eye

Happy man, woman, father
or ghost, time keeper, a
wreck, a saint, shuffler
or magnet, a day counter

And, so we talk it over.
But look at this night -
the clouds of this night
- moon hidden this night

Some courage

Here comes rain, and silt,
and heaven. Here gathers a
populace for a latest word
- ladies and gentleman, no
one will be forgotten. You
are here, too, not exactly
in a corner, but not quite
circulating, either. There
is the usual crew mustered
for uniformed combat; here
are tired eyes and dangled
hands - half-speeches from
broken chairs. In all this
what can I offer? No award
bears my name, no check is
forthcoming. I too am in a
tiring mode: is it courage
I lack to try the door, or
am I almost like a friend?

Friends

you are conscious
your saving grace
in a word as some
balsa wood castle

I too like you am
awake to accident
and utterance and
not a child alone

so they tell us a
story and vote so
you and I in turn
parting the cloth

even so the plans
& even thus rains
shadow their town
and down it falls

see that we marry
the eraser within
the path is clear
from self-erasure

an anonymous back
yard tree wave in
recollection when
it stripped today

all recollections
guests at a party
disappear & phase
into chairs again

I am glad for the
bright spark in a
dark circus spoke
my wandering pony

they appear in an
accident they are
like us in a dark
return of oneself

There'm I holding
now a soakt cloth
light thru a dust
centuries hanging

They too a finger
on a stone and as
well love-making,
speech lead to it

Thank you earth a
day so bright and
Part the guests a
bride who appears

I was saying this
is enough, Bright
applause somebody
the ladle dropped

There no accident
I felt in a spine
all accustomed to
bordered highways

leaf upon leaf is
dirt from dirt we
travel together I
see I am with you

in a magazine say
of poetry guess &
dollar for dollar
distant thrumming

Just like painted
canvas turning to
the wall recovers
darkness abrading

Subtlety the fawn
reasoning in hoof
stirred at a moss
tender in shadows

Speech is not one
a squirrel barked
& into a meadow a
patio and squares

I do not give you
over unremembered
I am apparent but
that without your

distance clearing
Hollow log signal
from night as day
brushes into view

A single disk the
sky speaks & bars
of darkness hover
We changed speech

& we changed too.
Needful cities by
turnpikes line up
gray prospectuses

X years have been
dark and required
just my attention
just some spark -

How'ill we say we
were here 'n mean
it How will we be
constant friends?

Anon.

                    House
                    and a
                    title
                    for I
                    alter
                    works

Guests

Day has arrived on my doorstep,
bag in hand - will it be a long
stay? Sitting side-by-side on a
sofa, I set aside from the bag:
a blade of grass, a harmonica -
each item prompts a story - how
day found a house, a girl, gray
nights drowning in number music
- a pin, a magnetic letter - by
turns an item & an explanation.

So simple the morning: the bed,
the stairs, the cereal. Now day
seems too busy for me, carrying
other negotiations. I am light,
but I will not wait forever. We
who disappear need something in
place of monuments: say I am no
longer alone and tiring; say we
overshot ourselves, but tonight
- candlelight and the veranda -

Day's afternoon

Someone familiar drifts into
view. It is day, grinning as
it hurriedly shoves some few
personal things out of being

Day is the thought I had for
a disinterested friend. Or a
background for the lines you
and I draw in love, or, this

was not day, not quite, this
is consciousness of a fallen
heart risen to its height. I
see the distinction, decide:

day is at the back of a yard
clearly awake, hands clasped
behind his back. I can leave
him there, no harm in that -

I can go do something else -
but I pause here too long to
get started on something new
- I am like that, I see, now

Poems for Days

Some again, sun

How you fell where
furious - my fight
without friendship

Tambourines rattle
clatter like stone
birds in the story

from left to right
and back again - I
too am reading in.

And you, becoming.
A poem in a room a
poem absent tunes.

That in its place - this
in a wooded valley. This
quietness not of place -
trees, creatures, filter
and obscure. So I notice
things I will not recall
waking - but I imagine a
twig snapping. Certainly
I have broken things. We
in a city do not stop at
magic & are not stopped.

The rail

A narrow rail in the
dusk, or when a calm
day is passing while
we catch up on work.

This is a correction
to work not done, to
carelessness, to our
time at arm's length

The sound is clearer
the voices quieter -
each of us intent as
day corrects itself.

Then we surrender, &
rubbing eyes we rise
and come on out into
a threading darkness

Academic

For some time now
a philosophy held
a head positioned
at a right angle.

I have an account
not a collection:
the wind swirling
while the body in

a circle. And you
can be saved from
everything but my
philosophy, I say

So the money grew
- and people come
to sit awhile and
the noises lessen

That's how a fall
made no noise. We
are fitted to our
medal as we sleep

And, waking, what
voice will suffer
for body miscast?
Do words suffice?

White Chef's Hat

Who is sensible?
Fire is sensible
if by sensible I
lean & surrender

White chef's hat
at the edge of a
river touching @
fresh mown grass

Walk with me and
touch the houses
whose fires ruin
a gentle evening

By sensible I am
all yours for an
open-ending talk
surrounding fire

Reading Twice

Everybody is right
in a world I can't
comprehend. Shapes
not words - colors
not sense. We fall
to our feet echoes
to aloneness. Will
I distract and win
a table? He cannot
win who won't hear
others' footsteps.

Read this first

Perhaps I could speak over
my shoulder. I could speak
from the distance, as on a
beach. Or from looking up,
or from looking down. What
difference should it make?
However I calculate cannot
guarantee me my listeners.
Speak as you must and wait
for no one looking for you

Lose at the Beach

Words for the beach are
lost at the beach. Feet
kick them loose or bury
them further along. Our
words are no less able.
I love you, here may be
lost at the beach there
- the wind is constant,
true, more than I. Also
these plastic toys seem
brighter, but fragile -
so there can be no cure
for what is lost at the
beach. Still we pack up
and go to the beach, to
lose what we can afford
to lose no other where.

Afterwards

> Words for the day elude me
> staying out of sight, then
> convening when I tire, the
> words loose in daylight...
> a bus ride downtown - some
> shopping - a free concert.
> All this time I am resting
> with other work. I wake to
> words on my floor, draping
> over the light fixtures...
> which is not to say I have
> no time for other people -

Dream About

Someone spoke of heaven
- & as I looked up from
my shoes I was suddenly
looking down on my self
from a startling height
so I had to stop myself
from lifting or holding
my self up to my face -
the face of my self was
tear-streaked and tired
while I felt calm. Then
my father was speaking,
from a corner, quietly,
calmly, in my voice. It
was interesting to hear
my voice like that - we
were a certain distance
apart, & we fell asleep
that way. When I woke -
my self, my child, wide
awake, was playing, and
he gave me a big smile.
My father was not there
anymore. The corner was
streaked with light, it
had been so dark, & now
light mingled the dust,
and I was tempted to go
over and look up to the
light, but I stood like
I had been standing, as
my child played and now
& then asked a question

The sleeping cat

The work went away. The cat
slept through my work shown
the door. Wish it well. You
have your arguments. We and
the cat can abide change. I
am not ruined, being myself
- I am not lost being quiet
in the public ear. And work
crossed the fields, perhaps
to a neighbor's table. They
will welcome a life by name
of work, and when they tire
of false names for desire -
work for poetry - work will
knock on some other's door,
tracing smoke from chimneys

Saturday

I am making something
out of nothing again,

or, what is truthful.
So another pale shirt

the rain will launder
- or - the rain steps

into a critical angle
- or - the wind stops

at toppling leaves, a
season soon arrested.

But enough of this. I
have an hour or so to

draw my narrow lines.

Say this last

The easiest day is the last day,
with all the other days behind -
hour stepping after hour, little
bridesmaids. You look up at blue
sky and are no closer. So, these
hands - waiting yet for profound
words dedicated to what hands do
- they can wait. Will you say to
yourself, one last time across a
lawn, one moment for my kitchen?
I think not. No. Now I see. Yes.
I was right to stay in my place.

Career posting

All this pressure - The
atmospheres on an empty
head - empty from labor
for a home to cradle it

And blamelessness - God
look on me for my proof
- I expect I just might
be speechless that soon

Won't we be a sight: in
the shadows of heaven -
a less transfixed light
- the first interview -

The Conductor

I have made a memory
and when I step back
and aside the memory
sparkling & vanishes

Alone I am free this
moment I tolerate my
disappearance when I
strike down by words

The moments I extend
for the work of this
record in leaves now
clipped, in a drawer

Vanished the work we
remember free for my
disappearance, where
struck down by words

Here is the equality
of morning light and
soaking rain and one
child to a big house

So he said Chapters,
and an old conductor
at his music wearily
under cloud of night

www.ingramcontent.com/pod-product-compliance
Lightning Source LLC
Chambersburg PA
CBHW031334040426
42443CB00005B/347